The Acorn House Bakery
Recipe Book

by

Helen Hermanstein Smith

begin a book Independent Publishers

begin a book

Book Cover by AnnMarie Reynolds for *begin a book*

Portrait Photography by © Graham Hiscock at www.studiohphotography.co.uk

Food/Recipe Photography by © Helen Hermanstein Smith

First edition printed in the United Kingdom 2023

ISBN (Print Paperback) 978-1-915353-13-9

Published by *begin a book Independent Publishers* who should be approached in the first instance for all copyright/rights queries.
www.beginabook.com/info@beginabook.com

For Derek, Charlotte and Adam

Introduction

My interest in baking dates back to when I was a small child growing up in a household filled with the delicious scent of freshly baked bread and cakes, these lovingly created by my mother and grandmother who always seemed to be baking. With homemade treats regularly on offer, baking became a normal part of my life and I genuinely thought it was how everyone lived.

My mother would bake bread for our large family every Saturday afternoon and, as a treat, she would also bake a fruit cake or sponge cake that we could eat on Sundays. As children, my siblings and I would be allowed to have a small piece of bread dough that we could shape into our very own 'loaf' of bread which I absolutely loved! It wasn't until I was about 9 years old that I realised most people bought their bread from the supermarket - wrapped in plastic.

I started baking cakes at about the age of 13 and this is when I made my very first fruit cake. After that I was seized by the baking bug. Friends and family began to enjoy my cakes and I started to receive a steady stream of commissions over many years which allowed me to hone my skills across different techniques.

Baking, though, remained a hobby as I developed my career in the technology world, working amongst computers and mobile phones whilst raising our two children. After many years in this industry I decided I wanted a change and naturally turned to baking as a new career. I trained in patisserie, bread baking, cake decorating and chocolate making at both the Westminster Kingsway College and Le Cordon Bleu School in London, eventually going on to become a qualified baker.

A few years ago I started my home baking business, Acorn House Bakery, and began to curate a collection of my tried and tested recipes from both my childhood and professional training. This book is the culmination of this collection and in creating each of the recipes I have taken inspriation from my mother. Her early influence is such a huge part of my baking today and I am so proud to own her little booklet of handwritten recipes. When she sadly died a couple of years ago it was in baking I sought solace, not only to help deal with my grief and loss, but also to bring back many happy memories of our times baking together.

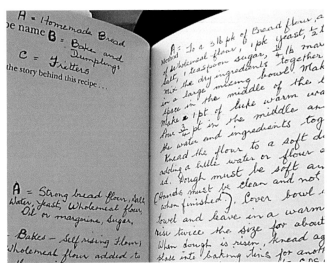

Collecting these recipes proved to be more challenging than I originally expected - I found I had so many in my head, that I needed to be really firm when choosing which recipes to include. In order to help with this selection, I decided to arrange them in a way that allows for all of the necessary techniques of successful home baking to be explored. I am thrilled now to have brought them all together in one place and am delighted to share my first compendium of recipes in this book. You will find both sweet and savoury delights, which offers something for everyone to enjoy.

In line with my heritage and passion, this book concentrates primarily on baking elements but I have thrown in the odd confectionary recipe or two for extra sweetness and variation. Don't be shy to experiment. Use these recipes as a great starting point and put your own twist, signature or stamp on them.

I hope you enjoy making these recipes as much as I have done and I hope that my passion for baking, passed down through the generations, will inspire you to fire up your oven and have a go!

Happy Baking!

Love Helen x

Contents

acorn house
bakery

Cookies & Sweet Treats

Cakes, Sponges & Scones

(Recipes titled 'AHB' are from my own Acorn House Bakery collection)

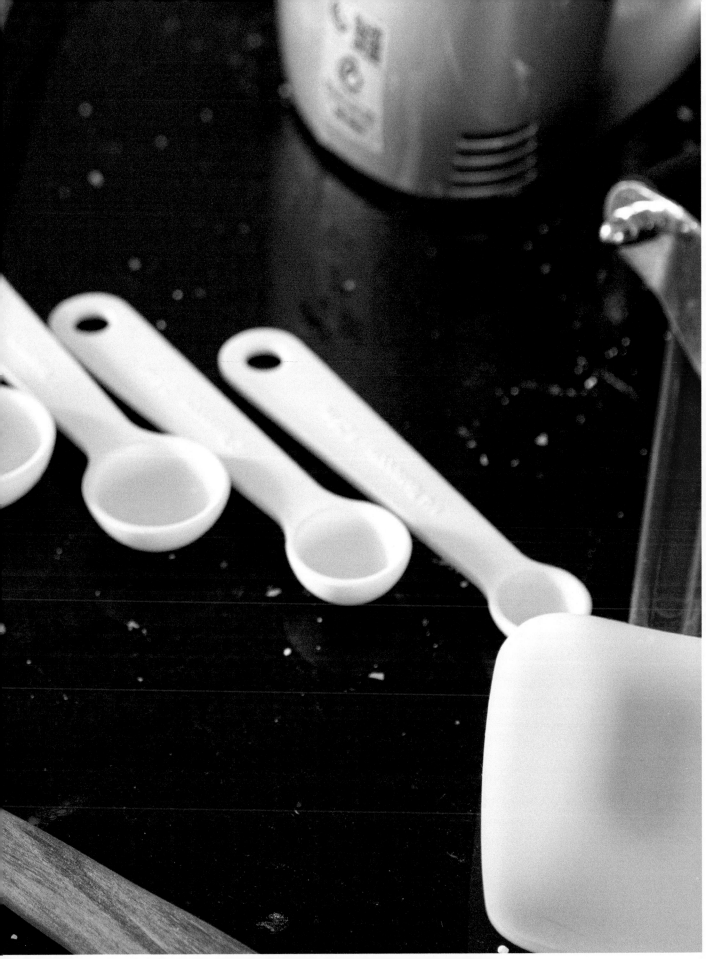

Notes, Tips & Hacks

Notes:

All of the recipes in this book use metric measurements. If you are not used to metric measures, I've included a handy conversion table on the opposite page.

All recipe temperatures stated are for a fan-assisted oven, however, as oven manufacturers differ, you should refer to your oven manufacturer's instruction manual for guidance. This is especially important if you are using a conventional oven as opposed to a fan oven.

Regular baking with your own oven will help you to become more familiar with how your oven bakes at different temperatures.

Tips & Hacks:

Here are some tips and hacks I use that I would love to share which will help to enhance your baking and cooking. I haven't written them in any particular order, so you can simply dip in and out of this list. Read through and maybe give some of them a try - you might find them really useful.

Oven Temperature

It's a good idea to get to know your oven. Does it tend to brown your bakes too quickly? Do your cakes bake with a dome in the middle? The reason for this could be that your oven cooks at a slightly hotter temperature than others (or the value stated in the recipe), so you should adjust the temperature accordingly. If your recipe says bake at 180°C, for example, try baking at 170°C instead. Also, if your oven has a temperature control dial and not a digital one, it is often very hard to set the temperature correctly. A little trial and error is needed to get to know the correct temperature setting on your oven.

Some ovens have a 'hot spot' (mine definitely does), where your bakes tend to brown more than in other parts of the oven. Bear this in mind when using up all the shelf space in your oven. If you find a 'hot spot' it is a good idea to rotate the baking tins or baking trays during baking.

Always make sure to pre-heat your oven at least 10 minutes prior to putting your uncooked ingredients in to bake, so that the oven can reach the correct temperature. For some ovens this pre-heat may be longer than 10 mins, depending upon the make and model. If you don't pre-heat the oven before baking, you may end up with a stodgy, undercooked result.

Conversion Table				
Weight		Temperature		
Metric	Imperial	Celsius	Fahrenheit	Gas
15 g	½ oz	50°C	125°F	0
30 g	1 oz	75°C	165°F	0
60 g	2 oz	80°C	175°F	0
85 g	3 oz	90°C	195°F	0
115 g	4 oz (1/4 lb)	100°C	210°F	0
140 g	5 oz	120°C	250°C	0.25
170 g	6 oz	130°C	265°F	0.5
200 g	7 oz	140°C	285°F	1
225 g	8 oz (1/2 lb)	150°C	300°F	2
255 g	9 oz	160°C	320°F	2
285 g	10 oz	170°C	340°F	3
310 g	11 oz	175°C	345°F	3
340 g	12 oz	180°C	355°F	4
370 g	13 oz	190°C	375°F	4
400 g	14 oz	200°F	400°F	5
425 g	15 oz	210°C	410°F	6
450 g	1 lb	220°C	425°F	7
680 g	1½ lbs	230°C	450°F	7
1 kg	2 lbs 3 oz	240°C	465°F	8

Testing your bakes

When testing a cake to see if it is fully cooked, I always use a bamboo skewer instead of a metal cake tester. I find that the skewer - being thicker than the thin metal tester - is better at showing whether the cake is cooked or not. These are inexpensive and well worth using.

For the perfect sponge cake

As a rule of thumb, I always use equal amounts of flour, sugar and softened butter/margarine. For the eggs, I tend to add roughly the same weight as that for the other individual ingredients. So, if you're adding 200g of flour and 200g of sugar, you would add 200g in weight of eggs. Weigh the whole eggs (in their shells) to approximate the weight required. It's okay for the weight to vary by a few grams. Weigh them in a separate bowl before adding them to your mixture then, mix all of the ingredients together at the same time.

Eggs should always be used at room temperature. If you are storing eggs in the fridge, make sure you take them out and give them enough time to come up to room temperature (usually about an hour) before adding them to your bakes. It really will make a difference to the rising of your sponges.

Handy hint: if you're using ounces, whatever that number is, halve it to give you the number of eggs to use. Always sift your flour and don't forget to make sure those eggs are at room temperature.

Preparing baking tins for cakes

Some bakers grease and flour their baking tins for cakes, however I always line my tins with baking parchment. For round tins, I place the baking tin on the baking parchment and draw a circle about 1cm larger than the tin and cut it out. Then I cut a long strip, the width of which should be about 2cm more than the depth of the tin and the length slightly more than the circumference of the tin. Cut a few 1cm slits around the edge of the round piece of baking parchment and place inside the baking tin then use the long strip to line the inner side of the baking tin. Your tin is now ready to use.

Perfecting shortcrust pastry

Is your pastry sometimes hard/dry/tasteless? Try using the 2:1 ratio of plain flour to butter and always use COLD butter - I often use frozen. Though cold or frozen butter can be hard to rub in, the trick is to grate it. That way you'll have very cold butter, but in very small pieces which makes the rubbing in process much easier. Always use an egg as the liquid to bind your pastry mixture together. If the mixture is a little dry, add cold water - a tbsp at a time.

Baking blind

Roll out your pastry and place it carefully into your flan/pie dish. Cut a piece of baking parchment or greaseproof paper large enough to cover the pastry in your flan/pie dish then scrunch up the paper before spreading it out. Cover the pastry with this paper and fill it with baking beans. I keep a bag of dried beans e.g. dried kidney beans or dried black eye beans for this, which can always be reused.

Trimming pastry from a flan/pie dish

When you place the pastry in your flan/pie dish, let the pastry hang over the edge. Use a rolling pin to roll over and press down
on the edge of the dish, until all of the excess pastry has been cut off. This will give you a perfectly trimmed edge.

Baking a flan/tart with a pastry base - but not baking blind

Place an upturned baking tray in the oven when you pre-heat it. Leave the upturned baking tray in the oven when it has
reached the required temperature and then place your flan or tart directly on top of this hot upturned baking tray. The direct heat from the tray will help prevent your flan or tart having a soggy bottom.

Rolling out pastry

Many people add flour to the work surface prior to rolling out pastry or dough which can sometimes change the consistency of the pastry or dough, making it dry. I often dust the rolling pin and my hands with a little flour instead.

Also, try rolling your pastry or dough in-between two large pieces of cling film. If the pastry or dough is not too wet it won't stick and you will avoid the problem of your pastry drying out (which can happen when using flour). You can also invest in a pastry mat. These are very useful and inexpensive.

Glazing your pastry

A glossy baked pastry can be achieved by glazing the pastry with a whisked egg before you bake it. For a shiny glaze: if you're baking for a short time, say up to 30 mins, use only the egg yolk but if you're baking for longer, use the whole egg.

Storing sugar

Does your unused sugar go hard if left in the packet? If you place the bag of sugar in a ziplock or sealed food bag, squeeze out the excess air and put it in the crisper drawer of your fridge, the moisture of the fridge will keep it lump free.

Cooking with crème fraîche

I tend to use crème fraîche in my recipes instead of cream (when cream is required) because I find that it tends to work better and gives a smoother, creamier mixture. Crème fraiche is made in the traditional way by skimming the cream off the milk, adding lactic cultures and then leaving the cream to slowly pasteurise at a low temperature. This method allows it to thicken into a smooth silky delicious cream with a distinctive rich taste. If you would like to try it, the best crème fraiche, the one I always use, is Isigny Sainte-Mère.

Sauces

When making sauces, if you find that your sauce develops lumps, don't despair, simply stir it with a whisk until the lumps disappear. This method can also be used when mixing powders, such as icing sugar or flour into liquid.

Happy Baking!

LIGHT
SAVOURY
SNACKS

acorn house
bakery

COURGETTE & FETA MUFFINS

Savoury muffins do sound strange - usually we expect muffins to be sweet - however I first came across savoury muffins some time ago and really liked the alternative flavour, so I decided to modify the sweet version of one of my muffin recipes. This resulted in a delicious savoury tea-time snack.

They remind me of a similar childhood snack my mother used to make that we would have warm served with baked beans. It was always a delicious treat.

Have a go at making these. You'll be blown away with how easy they are!

Courgette & Feta Muffins

Makes 12 large muffins

400g self-raising flour

2 tsp baking powder

1 tsp bicarbonate of soda

¼ tsp sea salt

1 tsp cumin seeds

2 large eggs

300ml buttermilk

10 tbsp sunflower oil

2 small courgettes (about 280g) grated and squeezed (in kitchen paper or a clean tea towel) to remove any liquid

200g feta cheese crumbled, or grated Parmesan, or grated Comté

Freeze dried parsley for sprinkling

acorn house
bakery

1. Heat oven to 180°C.
2. Line a large 12 hole muffin tray with paper cases, or you can use a silicon muffin tray which doesn't have to be lined.
3. In a large mixing bowl, sift the flour, baking powder, bicarbonate of soda and ¼ tsp salt together, add cumin seeds and mix these dry ingredients with a large spoon.
4. In a measuring jug, whisk together the eggs, buttermilk and oil until well combined.
5. Pour the wet ingredients into the dry ingredients and add the grated courgettes and half the crumbled feta (or other cheese). Stir to just combine - don't overmix (as this will toughen the texture of your baked muffins).
6. Divide the mixture between the muffin cases and top with the remaining feta (or other cheese) and a pinch of the dried parsley to garnish.
7. Bake for 25-30 mins until golden brown. A bamboo skewer inserted to the centre of a muffin should come out clean and dry when the muffins are cooked.
8. Place on a wire rack to cool. Can be eaten warm or cold.
9. These will keep for 2 days in an airtight container and a few days longer if refrigerated.

Note: These muffins are perfect served warm as a vegetarian snack with a slice of ham and salad for a light lunch, a tea time snack (with or without jam) or as part of a picnic. They can be served warm or cold.

As an alternative to courgette and feta you could use:
~ spinach & blue cheese
~ garden peas & tinned sweetcorn
~ bacon & sweet potato

EASY PLAITED LOAF BREAD

Making bread is not difficult, contrary to what some people think. Many shy away from making their own bread because they think it's all too much faff when a shop-bought loaf will do. Just the thought of kneading the dough, proving and waiting for it to rise can put people off and I get that, however if you have a bread making machine you can disregard this myth. You don't always have to settle for a shop-bought loaf - how about creating a show-stopping plaited loaf? Try this easy recipe and see what you can produce. You'll be surprised when you find out how easy it is.

Easy Plaited Loaf Bread

This recipe uses a bread making machine to make the dough.

Makes 1 loaf

450g strong bread flour

1 sachet (7g) quick instant dried yeast

6g sea salt

15g sugar

300ml tepid water

60ml olive oil

For glazing/decoration:

1 egg, lightly beaten

1 tbsp sesame seeds

Tip: Have half a cup of cool water ready next to the oven just before you put the bread dough in. As soon as you have put the bread dough into the oven, before closing the oven door, quickly throw the cup of water onto the base of the oven, avoiding the bread dough. Immediately shut the oven door. This creates a body of steam in the oven, that raises the temperature and creates a lovely crust on your bread!

acorn house bakery

1. Place the liquid ingredients, except the beaten egg, into the bread making machine.
2. Add the sugar and salt and stir to dissolve.
3. Add the flour, then sprinkle the dried yeast on top of the flour. Make sure the yeast does not touch the salt as this will kill the yeast.
4. Set the bread making machine to the 'Dough' setting to make the bread dough.
5. When the machine has made the dough, turn it out onto a lightly floured work surface.
6. Divide the dough into 3 equal parts and roll each of them into a sausage.
7. Lay each sausage shaped piece of dough vertically in front of you, and press the ends furthest, away from you, together. The ends nearest to you should be spaced apart.
8. Create a plait with the 3 pieces of dough, by alternatively placing the outer left-hand strand of dough into the middle and then the outer right hand strand into the middle. Continue until you have created a plait. Pinch the ends together and tuck under the end of the loaf.
9. Place on a floured baking tray and put in a warm place to allow the dough to double in size. This should take about 30-45mins.
10. Heat the oven to 220°C.
11. Brush the top of the loaf with the beaten egg and sprinkle with sesame seeds.
12. Bake in the oven for 12-15mins, or until it is a dark golden brown. The loaf will be done if, when tapped on the bottom, it makes the sound of a drum.
13. Place on a wire rack to cool.

Try adding some sundried tomatoes or some halved olives to the dough during the last 10 minutes of the bread machine mixing cycle.

FILO PASTRY PARCELS

I first made these filo pastry parcels on a wet and windy day when I had very little fresh food left in my veg box and fridge but didn't want to go out shopping. Instead I gathered together what I could and found the ingredients for this recipe. These little morsels are great as a tasty snack but also make great finger food for serving with drinks. They look like tiny triangular parcels encased in crisp filo pastry. I always use shop bought filo pastry for convenience. You can really play around with your fillings as this is a versatile recipe. There are various filling options to choose from - pick your favourite!

Filo Pastry Parcels

1 pk Filo pastry sheets

30g Butter, melted, or veg oil spray

Optional fillings:

- 100g turkey mince with ½ finely chopped shallot; 1 crushed garlic clove; ½ tsp garam masala, pinch chilli flakes, salt & pepper; or
- 80g Feta cheese; 30g baby leaf spinach, chopped; black pepper; or
- 80g Ricotta cheese; 30g baby leaf spinach; salt and black pepper season; or
- 80g Goats cheese; 2 tsp cranberry sauce

1. Make your fillings:
   - Turkey mince: Fry mince and all other ingredients for about 15mins until cooked through. Set aside to cool.
   - Feta Cheese & Spinach: Chop feta cheese and mix with chopped baby leaf spinach. Season with freshly ground black pepper.
   - Ricotta Cheese & Spinach: Mix Ricotta cheese with baby leaf spinach. Season with salt and freshly ground black pepper.
   - Goats Cheese & Cranberry: Chop the goats cheese and gently mix in the cranberry sauce.
2. Line a large baking tray with greaseproof paper, baking parchment or tin foil.
3. Cut each filo pastry sheet lengthwise down the middle to form x2 strips (use 1 strip per filling).
4. Place a teaspoonful of mixture in the bottom left-hand corner, about 1cm from the bottom. Then fold the bottom right-hand corner of the pastry over the mixture towards the left-hand edge and brush with melted butter and seal edge down, to create a triangle. Take the bottom left-hand corner of the pastry and neatly fold over to meet the right-hand edge of the pastry strip, brush with melted butter and seal down.
5. Repeat this folding process all the way up the pastry until a samosa type triangle parcel has been created. Tuck in sharp corners and secure with a little melted butter.
6. Brush the completed triangular parcel with melted butter, or spray with oil and place on the baking tray.
7. Repeat steps 3 to 6 until you have assembled all of your pastry triangles.
8. Bake in the oven at 190°C for 15mins until golden brown.
9. Serve warm.

Additional alternative fillings are:
~ Halloumi & shredded savoy or hispi cabbage
~ Leftover boiled potatoes & garden peas or petit pois
~ Strips of chicken & leek

MINI BACON & BUTTERNUT SQUASH TARTS

A little similar to my recipe for Filo Pastry Parcels, these tasty little tarts are ideal for serving as finger food at parties or as a savoury bite to have with drinks. When baked they are best served warm but can also be served cold as picnic food.

These tarts are both versatile and easy to make. You can also spice them up by adding a few drops of Tabasco sauce during cooking or as a condiment.

Equally they are just as delicious eaten with your favourite chutney.

Mini Bacon & Butternut Squash Tarts

Makes 12

1 sheet ready-made Puff Pastry

2 tbsp Olive Oil

1 med onion, thinly sliced

2 garlic cloves, crushed or finely chopped

½ tsp sea salt

100g smoked streaky bacon, roughly chopped

125g butternut squash, grated

5g fresh flat leaf parsley, chopped (including stalks)

1 tsp mixed herbs

3 medium eggs, lightly beaten

¼ tsp Dijon mustard

100g double cream

60g Parmesan cheese, grated

1 small green chilli, chopped (optional)

acorn house
bakery

1. Heat oven to 190°C.
2. Grease a 12-hole large muffin tray with some vegetable oil or butter.
3. Add olive oil to a frying pan and fry the onions, garlic, bacon, butternut squash (and chilli, if using) and mixed herbs over a high heat for about 6-8mins. Keep stirring until cooked. Set aside.
4. In a medium sized mixing bowl, using a whisk, mix together the eggs, cream, mustard and salt, until well combined.
5. Stir in the grated Parmesan cheese.
6. Add the bacon and vegetable mix to the egg and cream mixture and stir with a large spoon until it is all mixed together.
7. Cut pastry into 12 squares and place in the greased sections of the muffin tray. The corners will be poking out of the top, but this does not matter.
8. Carefully spoon the filling mixture into the pastry cases and sprinkle with the chopped fresh flat leaf parsley.
9. Bake for 20mins or until golden brown and the pastry is cooked.
10. Serve with a salad for lunch or as a snack with drinks.
11. Can be served warm or cold.

Alternative fillings you can use:
~ Chicken & sweet potato
~ Blue cheese & broccoli

PARMESAN SHORTBREAD

Whoever thought that shortbread could be eaten as a savoury biscuit?

If you like Parmesan, you'll really love these. They are absolutely delicious and make a great savoury bite to serve guests with at a party ... if they can last
that long!

These are also great served with cheese and a fruity chutney and make a great alternative to crackers. Or you can simply eat them on their own.

Parmesan Shortbread

Makes about 25

100g plain flour
75g butter
75g parmesan cheese, grated
1 tbsp dried thyme
½ tsp cayenne pepper

acorn house
bakery

1. Place all the ingredients into a food processor and mix until they form a dough. Alternatively, you can mix it by hand, rubbing all the ingredients together until they form a dough.
2. Roll the mixture into a sausage shape, approx 3cm in diameter and wrap tightly in clingfilm.
3. Place in the fridge to chill for at least 30mins. They can also stay in the fridge overnight.
4. Line a baking tray with baking parchment.
5. Remove the dough from the fridge and carefully slice the roll into ½-1cm thick rounds and lay out on a baking tray.
6. Bake at 200°C for 10-12mins until the edges are slightly golden.
7. Remove from the oven and cool on a baking tray.
8. These may be kept in an airtight tin for 7-10 days (if you can resist eating them!).

AHB SAUSAGE PLAIT

This recipe takes the humble sausage roll to a whole new level. By using high quality sausage meat and mixing it with interesting and delicious flavours, you can create this warm and satisfying light 'anytime' meal. The puff pastry is cut to create the plait giving you a dish that looks like a work of art.

In this recipe I have used wild boar and cranberry sausage meat which is a favourite from my local butcher, however you can substitute the recipe with any speciality sausage. All you have to do is squeeze the meat out of your favourite sausage and mix it with your preferred flavourings.

acorn house
bakery

AHB Sausage Plait

Serves 4

1 sheet ready-made puff pastry; keep in fridge until ready to use

500g speciality sausages*: skins removed

1 egg, beaten

½ tsp dried mixed herbs

Plain flour for rolling out

*Options: Cumberland or Lincolnshire Sausages can be used

acorn house
bakery

1. Pre-heat oven to 180°C.
2. Line a baking tray with baking parchment or greaseproof paper.
3. Skin sausages and put sausagemeat, dried herbs and sweet chilli sauce (if using) into a mixing bowl. Mix together using a fork. Set aside.
4. Take pastry out of fridge and lay it out on your work surface, lightly dusted with some of the plain flour.
5. Make sure the pastry is oblong shaped with the short sides at the top and bottom.
6. Lightly mark x2 lines (with the back of a blunt knife), on the pastry, creating 3 equal columns.
7. Using a pastry brush, brush some of the beaten egg all over the pastry.
8. Spread the sausagemeat evenly all down the middle column of the pastry sheet. It doesn't matter if it doesn't go all the way to the top and bottom edges.
9. Using a sharp knife, cut lines at a slight upward angle down the right hand and left hand columns of the pastry sheet.
10. Carefully cover the sausagemeat with alternate strips of the pastry, folding them inwards all the way down to create a 'plait', until you have covered all the sausage mixture. It doesn't matter if some of the mixture can be seen at the top and bottom or the sides.
11. Brush the 'plait' with the remaining beaten egg.
12. Bake in the oven for 45-50 minutes until golden brown.
13. Serve warm with a salad or boiled new potatoes with butter and fresh leaf parsley.

Try adding additional flavours to your sausage meat:
- Chilli flakes
- Dried herbs
- Fennel seeds
- Chutney
- Grated cheese

FLANS & TARTS

APRICOT & ALMOND TART

I think apricots and almonds are a match made in heaven when it comes to desserts. Apricots bring both a delicious tart and sweet sensation to this summery dessert. In this recipe, I have used both dried apricots and canned apricots as they are equally tasty when used in tarts. By using the two varieties of apricots, it allows you to make this summery recipe at any time of the year, without having to buy imported fresh ones out of season. When I was a child growing up, my mother would often use canned fruits that were out of season to make colourful desserts during the winter months. These desserts would brighten up a cold dark afternoon.

acorn house
bakery

Apricot & Almond Tart

Serves 8

Pastry:
140g plain flour
30g ground almonds
85g butter (best chilled and chopped)
1 medium egg (slightly beaten)
1 egg white

Apricot Filling:
250g – 300g soft dried apricots (chopped) (Malatya are best)
15ml lemon juice
45-60ml water
Few drops of vanilla extract
2 capfuls of Amaretto (optional)

Sponge:
160g Self raising flour
50g ground almonds
170g butter (softened)
170g castor sugar
3 eggs
5ml almond extract

Topping:
1 can apricots halves (in juice), drained
A generous handful of flaked almonds to decorate

1. Make the Pastry: Mix flour and ground almonds together in a mixing bowl. Rub in chilled butter with fingertips, until it resembles fine breadcrumbs. Stir in beaten egg with a fork and bring together, using your hands, into a ball of dough. Flatten to a disk shape, wrap in cling film and place in fridge to rest and chill for up to 15mins.

2. Make the filling: Put chopped dried apricots, lemon juice, water, and Amaretto (if using) into a saucepan and simmer until very soft and swollen (about 10mins). Set aside and leave to cool.

3. Place an upturned baking tray in oven and heat oven to 180°C. Leave upturned baking tray in the oven. The tart will cook on top of this to avoid having a 'soggy bottom'. Take the pastry dough out of the fridge and allow to come back to room temperature (makes it easier to roll out).

4. Roll out pastry on a lightly floured board and line 23cm flan dish. Any shallow dish will do if you don't have a flan dish. Cover pastry with baking parchment or greaseproof paper and fill with baking beans (any dried beans will do). Bake in oven for 15mins. Remove baking beans and paper, brush with the egg white and return to oven for a further 5 mins. When done, remove and leave to cool slightly. Turn the oven down to 170°C.

5. Take the apricot filling mixture, and using a hand blender or large fork to blend/mash it until there are only a few apricots lumps left in it. It doesn't have to be a smooth mixture. Add the vanilla essence (and Amaretto if using) and stir well. Set aside.

6. Make the sponge: Place all the sponge ingredients in a mixing bowl and mix together until well combined. A hand mixer is best for this, but a wooden spoon is adequate.

7. Take the apricot mixture and spread it over the pastry in the flan dish. Then spoon the sponge mixture carefully on top of the apricot mixture.

For a variation on this recipe, you could add 2 tbsp of dark rum to the canned apricots. This will give a delicious kick to your dessert.

Apricot & Almond Tart
(continued)

8. For the topping, place the apricot halves, cut side down, evenly on top of the sponge mixture. Sprinkle the flaked almonds on top.

9. Bake in the oven for around 40-45 minutes until golden brown. Test the sponge with a bamboo skewer (it's better than a cake tester) to make sure sponge is cooked. Bake a little longer if required. Hint: only stick the skewer into the sponge at an angle to test. If it goes into the apricot mixture the skewer comes out sticky and the flan will always appear uncooked.

10. Served warm with double cream or crème fraîche.

acorn house
bakery

BAKEWELL TART

Bakewell is a market town in Derbyshire. Folklore has it that a pub landlord asked his cook to make a sponge and some jam tarts. The result was a mixture of the two – obviously with the addition of almond flavouring! This tart is a traditional favourite, now topped with fondant icing. It is a treat that can be eaten as a dessert or with a cup of tea. But to be honest, you'll find yourself just eating it at any time you like, as a lovely, sweet treat.

Bakewell Tart

Serves 4

Pastry
140g plain flour
30g ground almonds
85g butter (best chilled and chopped)
1 medium egg (slightly beaten)

Filling
130g raspberry jam
1 tsp almond extract

Topping
115g butter
115g castor sugar
60g self-raising flour
60g ground almonds
2 medium eggs

Icing
170g icing sugar
6 tsp cooled boiled water, more if necessary
½ tsp almond extract
3 glace cherries

1. Make Pastry: Mix flour and ground almonds together in a mixing bowl. Rub in chilled butter, with fingertips until it resembles fine breadcrumbs. Stir in beaten egg with a fork and bring together into a ball of dough. Flatten to a disk shape, wrap in cling film and place in fridge to rest and chill for up to 15mins.

2. Place an upturned baking tray in the oven and heat oven to 180°C. Leave the upturned baking tray in the oven.

3. Roll out pastry on a lightly floured board and line 15cm flan tin.

4. Make Sponge: Using a wooden spoon, mix all sponge ingredients together in a very large bowl, until well combined. Set aside.

5. Prepare Filling: Mix raspberry jam and almond extract and spread evenly over the pastry.

6. Spread sponge mixture evenly over jam, making sure it touches the pastry.

7. Place in the oven on top of the hot upturned tray and bake in oven for 45mins or until golden brown and cooked. The upturned tray helps prevent your tart having a soggy bottom. When the tart is cooked, remove from the oven and leave to cool on a cooling rack.

8. Make Icing Topping: When the tart is completely cool, make icing topping by gradually adding a little cooled boiled water to the icing sugar, a teaspoon at a time, until a thick spreading consistency is achieved. Add the almond extract to flavour.

9. Pour over the top of the cooled tart, spreading evenly with a knife, occasionally dipped in hot water to help spread the icing.

10. Place 3 glace cherries on top in the middle and leave to set. Serve and enjoy!

If you prefer not to have icing on top of your Bakewell tart, try scattering some flaked almonds on top of the sponge mixture prior to baking, instead..

PLUM & ALMOND FRANGIPANE TART

Frangipane is basically an almond flavoured sponge, made with a combination of ground almonds and flour. This type of sponge mix is widely used in French patisserie tarts and is great in sweet tart recipes where seasonal summer stoned fruits are used, but you can also use pears and apples.

This is a frangipane recipe I would always make when we stayed at our holiday villa in the South of France. The local seasonal summer plums were always perfect for this dessert.

It also works extremely well with English Victoria Plums.

This dessert is best served warm with a dollop of vanilla ice cream or crème fraîche.

acorn house
bakery

Plum & Almond Frangipane Tart

Serves 8

For the Pastry:
200g plain flour
50g ground almonds
125g cold butter, chopped into small pieces
50g golden caster sugar
1 egg, beaten

For the Frangipane:
170g self raising flour
50g ground almonds
170g butter (softened)
170g caster sugar
3 eggs
1 tsp almond extract

For the Frangipane Topping:
About 12 plums, halved and stoned
1 tsp golden caster sugar or icing sugar (unrefined, if possible)
½ tsp almond extract
A generous handful of flaked almonds to decorate

acorn house
bakery

1. Make pastry: Mix flour and ground almonds together in a mixing bowl. Rub in chilled butter, with fingertips until it resembles fine breadcrumbs. Add the caster sugar and mix well. Stir in beaten egg with a fork and bring together into a ball of dough. Flatten to a disk shape, wrap in cling film and place in fridge to rest and chill for up to 15mins.

2. Heat oven to 180°C.

3. Prepare the frangipane topping: Place plums in a medium sized bowl, sprinkle with sugar, add almond extract and stir with a spoon until the plums are evenly coated. Set aside.

4. Take pastry out of the fridge and roll out and line a 20-22cm flan dish. Any shallow dish will do, if you don't have a flan dish. Cover pastry with baking parchment or greaseproof paper and fill with baking beans (I keep a bag of dried beans – [dried kidney beans, dried black eye beans], for this, which can always be reused).

5. Put in the oven and bake for 15mins (blind baking).

6. Remove baking beans and paper and return the pastry to oven for a further 5 mins at 180°C.

7. When the pastry is done, remove and put to one side. Turn the oven down to 170°C.

8. Make the frangipane: Place all the frangipane topping ingredients together in a bowl. A hand mixer is best for this, but a wooden spoon is adequate. The mixture should be fairly thick. If too runny, add 1 heaped tbsp of ground almonds and mix in well.

9. Spoon the frangipane mixture onto the pastry and spread evenly over the top.

10. For the Frangipane Topping: Lay the plums cut side down skin side up neatly on top of the frangipane, making sure that there are not too many gaps. You can afford to really squash them together, as they will shrink when baked.

11. Sprinkle the flaked almonds on top of the plums and bake in the oven for 45-50mins, or more if needed, until thoroughly cooked. To test if it is cooked, insert a bamboo skewer or cake tester. If it comes out, it is cooked, if not, bake for a little longer.

12. Serve hot or cold with crème fraiche or ice cream.

Variations of fruit for this recipe:
~ Apples
~ Pears
~ Apricots
~ Cherries

SHALLOT TARTE TATIN

A tarte tatin does not always have to be sweet, as this recipe will show you. This is a savoury take on the traditional French recipe for apple tarte tatin, which I think works really well. It also looks amazing! If you want to be adventurous, give this one a try. You can make it with caramelised shallots, as I have done here or you can use, caramelised root vegetables or any leftover cooked veg that you may have in the fridge. People will ask "did you really make that?"...and you can say with confidence "yes I did!"

Shallot Tarte Tatin

Serves 4-6

320g puff pastry

4 tbsp sunflower oil

5-6 banana shallots, peeled, cut in half lengthways

3 tbsp soft light brown sugar

4 tbsp balsamic vinegar

2 tbsp brandy (optional)

2 fresh thyme sprigs & 1 fresh rosemary sprig

½ tsp sea salt flakes

½ tsp cracked black pepper

Plain flour for dusting

This recipe uses a 25cm non-stick frying pan which must be able to go in an oven.

1. Roll out the pastry on a lightly floured surface to around 4mm thick, then cut it into a circle measuring about 2.5cm larger in diameter than your frying pan.
2. Transfer the pastry circle to a baking tray lined with non-stick baking paper, then cover and chill until needed (at least 20 minutes).
3. Heat the oven to 170°C.
4. Heat 3 tbsps of sunflower oil in the frying pan over a medium heat.
5. Add the shallots, cut side up, making sure you have enough to cover the base.
6. Cook for 3-4 minutes, then sprinkle over the brown sugar. Carefully turn over the shallots using a palette knife – arrange them neatly so the base is covered and there aren't any gaps.
7. Turn down the heat to low, then add the balsamic vinegar and brandy, if using. (The alcohol will cook off, leaving behind just the brandy flavour).
8. Add the leaves from the sprigs of thyme and rosemary, and let the shallots caramelise for 4-5 minutes. Sprinkle with the salt and pepper, then turn off the heat and drizzle over the remaining oil.
9. Carefully lift the chilled pastry and lay it over the pan. Using a wooden spoon to carefully tuck the pastry over the shallots and right into the edges of the pan.
10. Put the frying pan into the oven and bake the tarte for 25-30 minutes or until the pastry is golden brown and cooked.
11. When cooked, USE OVEN GLOVES to remove from the oven. Using oven gloves, place a warmed plate (slightly larger than the frying pan) over the frying pan and quickly, but carefully* turn it over, so that the frying pan is upside down on top of the plate. The pastry side of the tart tatin will be on the plate with the shallots on top. Lift the frying pan off the plate.
12. Serve warm with salad or vegetables. Beware - the juices from the tart will be extremely hot because of the sugar used!

Alternative vegetables to use are:
~ Parsnips
~ Sweet potatoes
~ Butternut squash

TOMATO & FETA CHEESE TART

Who doesn't like a lovely colourful tart to adorn your lunch table? This recipe is not only colourful but also shouts 'summertime' whenever you bake it. Cherry tomatoes are used in this tart with Greek Feta cheese. I think that this combination works well. Complementing these two ingredients are green olives and sundried tomatoes making a scrumptious tart that can be eaten for a delicious vegetarian lunch with buttered new potatoes, with a salad or served as a light supper.

Either way, if you enjoy eating tomatoes and Feta cheese, you'll love this tart!

acorn house
bakery

Tomato & Feta Cheese Tart

Serves 4

1 sheet ready-rolled puff pastry (keep in the fridge until ready to use)

2 tbsp olive oil

2 rashers smoked bacon, roughly chopped

2 large banana shallots, finely chopped

1 tsp herbs de Provence

25 fresh cherry tomatoes, cut in half

6 sun dried tomatoes (in oil), cut into strips

15 green pitted olives, cut in half lengthways

150g Feta cheese, crumbled or cut into small pieces

This recipe requires x 2 baking trays.

1. Place a flat baking tray upside down on a shelf in the oven and pre heat oven to 200°C. The tart will cook on this upside-down baking tray to prevent it getting a soggy bottom.
2. Line another baking tray with baking parchment.
3. Heat the olive oil in a frying pan over a medium heat and fry the bacon for about 4 minutes.
4. Add the shallots and herbs and continue to fry for a further 4 minutes.
5. Remove from the heat and set aside to cool slightly.
6. Unroll the sheet of ready-rolled puff pastry and place onto the lined baking tray. Slightly turn up the sides of the pastry.
7. Spread the bacon and onion mixture evenly over the pastry.
8. Layer the olives, sundried tomatoes and cherry tomatoes over the top, then add the crumbled Feta cheese.
9. Bake for 35mins until golden.
10. Serve warm.

You can also use black olives or a combination of both black and green olives. Torn basil leaves are also great to put on as a garnish just before serving.

VEGETABLE & GOAT'S CHEESE FLAN

This is a great summer dish to share with friends. I absolutely love goat's cheese, and first had one of these flans in a local town we visit every year in the South of France. Each market day, locals would flock into town to buy their fresh produce for the week, however, before any shopping was done, they would stop, sit and have a coffee with a pastry. The cafés would only serve coffee (or Pastis) – so you had to buy your pastries separately at the boulangerie, to eat them at the café. I always chose a miniature version of this flan. This tart is great hot or cold served with crushed buttery new potatoes or with a salad.

Vegetable & Goat's Cheese Flan

Serves 4-6

Pastry:

170g plain flour

85g salted Butter (chilled and chopped)

20g parmesan cheese, finely grated

1 egg (slightly beaten)

Filling:

8 eggs

200g creme fraiche

125g goat's cheese

40g black olives

75g sundried tomatoes, cut into strips

½ red onion, thinly sliced

½ green chilli, deseeded and sliced

12 cherry tomatoes, cut into halves

2 tbsp flat leaf parsley, chopped

Salt and freshly ground black pepper

acorn house
bakery

1. Make pastry: Place the flour in a mixing bowl and rub in the chilled butter, using your fingertips until it resembles breadcrumbs. Add the Parmesan cheese and mix well. Using a fork, stir in the beaten egg gradually (you may not need all of it) and bring together into a ball of dough. Flatten to a disk shape, wrap in cling film and place in fridge to rest and chill for up to 15mins.

2. Place a flat baking tray upside down on a shelf in the oven and pre heat oven to 180°C. The tart will cook on this upside-down baking tray to prevent it getting a soggy bottom.

3. Take pastry out of the fridge and roll out and line a 20-22cm flan dish. Any shallow dish will do if you don't have a flan dish. Cover pastry with baking parchment or greaseproof paper and fill with baking beans (I keep a bag of dried beans for this, which can always be reused).

4. Put in the oven and blind bake for 15mins. Remove baking beans and paper and return to oven for a further 5 mins. When done, remove from the oven and leave to cool slightly. Turn the oven down to 170°C.

5. Prepare the filling: In a medium sized mixing bowl, whisk together the crème fraiche and eggs until well combined.

6. Stir in red onion, olives, sundried tomatoes and chilli and season with the salt and pepper.

7. Cut up goat's cheese and set aside.

8. Place the flan dish onto a baking tray and carefully pour the egg mixture into pastry case and place cherry tomatoes, cut side down evenly over the mixture.

9. Add the pieces of goat's cheese evenly into the mixture and sprinkle with the chopped parsley.

10. Bake in the oven for about 50mins, or until golden brown and cooked. The tart should have a very slight wobble when done, but not too much. It will solidify as it cools down.

11. When cooked, remove from the oven and allow to cool for at least 10mins.

12. Serve warm or cold with a salad or vegetables. Enjoy!

You can use whichever vegetables you like, that work well with goat's cheese.
If you don't like goat's cheese, you can substitute it for whatever cheese you prefer.

COOKIES & SWEET TREATS

acorn house
bakery

AHB CREAMY FUDGE

Fudge was first created not in the UK but in the USA in the late 1800's. Precise cooking times and measurements were used to make this deliciously sweet treat. It has been said that fudge was created by accident by a confectioner in Baltimore, USA who made a bad batch of caramel. He basically 'fudged' it and hence fudge was born! This is a great recipe for making homemade sweets. Using only 4 ingredients this is a foolproof recipe for fudge that will always give any sweet tooth a delicious result. You can add different flavours depending on what you prefer. When cut up and put into bags it makes a perfect edible gift too!

AHB Creamy Fudge

15g salted butter

1 can condensed milk

150ml double cream

500g Icing sugar, sifted

Optional flavouring:

Vanilla Flavour: 1 tsp vanilla extract

Chocolate flavour: 100g 50-60% dark chocolate, chopped, or add 20g cocoa powder to icing sugar (sifted)

Fruit & Nut Flavour: 50g mixture of chopped walnuts & raisins

Strawberry Flavour: 5g freeze dried strawberries

Raspberry Flavour: 5g freeze dried raspberries

Rum Flavour: 60ml dark Caribbean rum

Whisky Flavour: 85ml preferred whisky

Festive Flavour: 50g mixture of chopped pistachios and cranberries, or add dollops of mincemeat and press down into mixture.

This recipe requires the use of a sugar thermometer.

1. Line 20cm baking tin with baking parchment, making sure it comes up the sides by about 2 inches.
2. Melt butter in saucepan, add condensed milk and cream over a medium heat and stir together.
3. Add ½ the icing sugar
4. Stir with a large whisk until thoroughly mixed in. Make sure you stir and do not whisk!
5. Add remaining ½ of icing sugar and stir with whisk until all mixed in.
6. When all the icing sugar has been mixed in and dissolved, turn up the heat, bring the mixture to a rolling boil and heat to 112°C-115°C, whilst constantly stirring with the whisk or silicone spoon or wooden spoon.
7. It's done when mixture starts coming away from the sides and the bottom when stirred, and the above temperature has been reached.
8. Remove from heat and keep stirring slowly for a further 1 minute. [You can add your flavours at this stage. If adding alcohol, be careful, as mixture may spit when liquid is added].
9. If adding mincemeat, add after the mixture has been poured into the lined baking tin.
10. Pour mixture into the lined baking tin and allow to cool, then refrigerate overnight.
11. Remove from baking tin and cut up into smalls squares.

Note: This fudge can be put into small gift bags, tied with ribbon, and given out as party favours, edible gifts or wrapped in festive packaging, as presents for Christmas.

It is worth buying in a sugar thermometer for making these sweet treats. They are inexpensive and well worth the investment.

BISCOFF BROWNIES

Brownies are always great to have as a small afternoon sweet treat. Lotus Biscoff biscuits are thin and crunchy and have a caramelised cinnamon flavour. These biscuits are usually served with coffee in Europe. You will often find them being served as a single biscuit with coffee in the UK too. If you like Biscoff cookies, you'll love these.

These delicious brownies are not only yummy, but decadently chocolatey and packed with luscious pieces of Biscoff biscuits. Obviously these brownies are great with coffee,
tea, hot chocolate or just on their own or served warm as a dessert. You'll find it hard to resist eating just one.

Biscoff Brownies

Makes 12

150 g salted butter, melted

180 g soft light brown sugar

150 g golden caster sugar

3 large eggs, at room temperature

2 tsp vanilla extract

60 g cocoa powder

90 g self raising flour

200g Biscoff biscuits, roughly broken

200g Biscoff spread (I use the smooth spread)

50g white chocolate, broken into small pieces

1. Preheat your oven to 175°C.
2. Line a 20cm square baking tin with baking parchment and set aside.
3. In a large bowl, place melted butter and both sugars and mix together using a whisk, until well combined.
4. Add eggs and vanilla extract and mix again with the whisk to combine the ingredients.
5. Sift in the cocoa powder and flour and mix with the whisk until well combined.
6. Add the broken biscuits and white chocolate pieces and using a wooden spoon, gently stir into the mixture.
7. Pour the brownie batter into the lined baking tin.
8. Slightly warm the Biscoff spread in the microwave for about 15 secs. Stir the spread, then gently swirl it over and through the mixture, using a cocktail stick or bamboo skewer.
9. Put in the oven and bake for about 30-35 minutes, until the top is crisp and the middle still feels a little squishy under the crust.
10. Remove from the oven and cool completely in the baking tray before placing in the fridge for about 30mins to firm up.
11. To cut the brownies, run your knife under hot water for a few seconds, then cut the brownies into evenly sized squares.
12. The brownies can be eaten as they are or warmed slightly and served as a dessert with vanilla ice cream. Enjoy!

The Lotus Biscoff biscuits were first made in a Belgian local bakery in a town called Lembeke in 1932 and are now widely available across the UK. You can buy Lotus Biscoff: Cookies, Cookie Butter, Sandwich Cookies, Ice Cream and Chocolate.

CHOCOLATE & ALMOND COOKIES

These chocolate almond cookies are a classic Christmas cookie, which originated in Basel, Switzerland in the 1700s. They are traditionally called 'Basler Brunsli', 'brun' meaning brown and 'li' meaning small: small brown cookies.

The process of making these cookies involves leaving them uncovered, to dry out overnight.

This may seem like a strange procedure, but it is essential for creating their distinctive crisp outer shell and slightly chewy inner texture.

When baked, they can be packaged up, tied with a festive ribbon and given as beautiful festive gifts, or simply eaten as a treat with a cup of coffee or tea.

Chocolate & Almond Cookies

Makes approx. 30 cookies

100g almond flour (finely ground almonds in a food processor)
100g golden caster sugar, plus extra for rolling out and sprinkling
85g dark chocolate (min. 50% cocoa solids), chopped
½ tsp ground cinnamon
¼ tsp ground cloves
1 egg white

1. Put the almond flour, sugar, chopped chocolate, ground cinnamon and ground cloves in a food processor and process until you are left with a fine powder.
2. Add the egg white and pulse until everything combines.
3. Bring the dough together into a ball, using your hands.
4. Flatten the ball of dough slightly, wrap in clingfilm and chill for around 30 minutes. This makes the dough easier to work with later.
5. In the meantime, line a large baking tray with baking parchment.
6. Place a piece of parchment paper on your worktop. Sprinkle it with some of the extra castor sugar, flatten the dough a little, then sprinkle with a little more castor sugar on top. Cover with another piece of parchment paper then roll out to a thickness of about 4mm.
7. Remove the top layer of parchment paper and cut out shapes using a cookie cutter of your choice.
8. Transfer the cookies to the lined baking tray and leave to air dry for at least 3 hours or overnight. If leaving overnight, cover loosely with a clean kitchen towel.
9. Preheat the oven to 160°C and bake the cookies for around 12-15 minutes until the tops are gently puffed up and dry.
10. Leave to cool 5-10 minutes on the baking sheet before placing on a cooling rack.
11. When completely cool, the cookies can be stored in an airtight tin until needed. They should still be OK for 10-15 days.

Note:
The dough is supposed to be moist, but if you feel it is a little too wet, you can add a little more almond flour, if needed. The left-over cookie dough can be rolled out again to make more cookies.

As these cookies are made using ground almonds and no animal fat, they are both Gluten Free and Dairy Free.

CHOCOLATE TRUFFLES

Chocolate Truffles are basically thick solid chocolate ganache (traditionally a mixture of chocolate and cream), which is then rolled into balls, coated in cocoa powder, icing sugar or chopped nuts.

This basic recipe only requires two main ingredients, then you can add whatever flavourings you like! The name was given to them because they resembled the edible fungi called truffles. These are super easy to do and make wonderful chocolate gifts.

acorn house
bakery

Chocolate Truffles

Makes approx. 8-12 Truffles

200g dark chocolate
100g double cream

Coating options:
Cocoa powder
Freeze-dried strawberries
Freeze-dried raspberries
Finely chopped pistachios

A pair of disposable gloves is recommended for coating the chocolate truffles - this can be a very messy procedure!

acorn house
bakery

1. Coarsely chop the chocolate with a serrated knife.
2. Place in a heatproof bowl.
3. Pour the cream into a small saucepan and over a medium heat bring to almost boiling. Take off the heat as soon as small bubbles start to appear in the cream.
4. Wait 30 seconds, then pour the hot cream over the chopped chocolate and let stand for about 2 minutes to allow the hot cream to start to melt the chocolate.
5. With a spoon, stir the chocolate and cream, using a figure of 8 motion. This allows the chocolate to blend into the warm cream evenly, giving you a beautiful smooth mixture. It may look as if it is not mixing in properly but keep going and you'll eventually get there!
6. Once all the chocolate has been mixed in and you have a smooth silky mixture, set the bowl aside and allow it to cool. When cool, cover with cling film and place the bowl in the fridge for 2-3 hours to solidify, ready to make into truffles. I like to leave mine overnight!
7. Prepare your preferred coatings in saucers or ramekins and line a baking tray with baking parchment or greaseproof paper.
8. When the mixture is cold and firm, take it out of the fridge.
9. It helps to wear disposable gloves for this part! Using a melon baller (if unavailable a teaspoon will do), scoop out the ganache mixture into small balls.
10. Roll each ganache ball in your preferred coating until it is evenly coated, then place on the lined baking tray. When done, put in the fridge to firm up again.
11. The chocolate truffles can be served as petit fours with coffee or simply enjoyed as a chocolate treat.

CUSTARD CREAM BLONDIES

Most people have their favourite biscuit. These were my mother's favourites, so as a child growing up, we always had them in the biscuit tin. This recipe is really a homage to my childhood and the popular biscuit in my mother's biscuit tin. If you like custard cream biscuits, you will love these. They are a delicious alternative to the traditional brownie, but just as yummy and they can be enjoyed at any time – if they can stay around long enough!

Custard Cream Blondies

Makes 12 Blondies

200g butter

200g caster sugar

100g soft light brown sugar

4 tbsp custard powder

3 eggs

225g plain flour, sifted

1 tsp vanilla extract or vanilla bean paste

200g custard cream biscuits

150g white chocolate, chopped

1. Preheat the oven to 175°C.
2. Line a 20cm square baking tin with baking parchment.
3. Melt the butter gently in a saucepan over a low heat and allow to cool slightly.
4. In a large mixing bowl, add the caster sugar, soft brown sugar and custard powder. Use a balloon whisk and mix together. Make a well in the middle.
5. Pour the melted butter into the well and mix together with the whisk, until well combined.
6. Add the eggs one at a time and mix in with the whisk until the mixture is smooth and thick. Add the vanilla extract and mix in.
7. Add the sifted flour and, using a spatula, gently fold together until all combined.
8. Reserve about 12 custard cream biscuits to decorate blondies and break up the remaining biscuits into small pieces and add into the mixture.
9. Add the chopped white chocolate and then fold everything together.
10. Pour the batter into the lined baking tin and spread evenly.
11. Place the remaining custard creams biscuits on top of the blondie mixture, pushing them down slightly.
12. Bake for 45 minutes, until firm but still a bit soft in the centre.
13. When baked, leave the blondies in the baking tin to cool. When completely cool, place baking tin in the fridge for a couple of hours. This helps to firm them up and makes it easier to cut them up.
14. When firm, remove from the fridge and lift out of the baking tin. Place on a chopping board and allow to come to room temperature.
15. Cut up into squares, each with its own custard cream biscuit on it and... enjoy!

You can make this recipe using any of your favourite non-chocolate biscuits.

DOUBLE CHOCOLATE CHIP COOKIES

The chocolate chip cookie is a ubiquitous feature in the cookie world. You will always find them on offer in cafés and coffee shops. I have tried many and baked many, but these are without a doubt the most chocolatey chocolate chip cookies I have ever tasted! This, in my humble opinion, has to be the ultimate chocolate chip cookie recipe. For this recipe, I have used cocoa and dark chocolate chips to give it the double chocolate title. If you prefer milk chocolate, substitute the dark chocolate chips with milk chocolate chips. If you like chocolate chip cookies, you'll love making these.

Double Chocolate Chip Cookies

Makes 12 cookies

115g salted butter, softened

230g soft dark brown sugar

1 egg

1 tsp vanilla extract

230g plain flour

½ tsp baking soda

50g cocoa powder

1 tsp espresso coffee powder

½ tsp sea salt

150g dark chocolate chips

1. Preheat the oven to 170°C.
2. Line a baking sheet with parchment paper.
3. In a large mixing bowl, beat together the butter and sugar with an electric hand mixer or an electric food mixer. Beat for about 2-3minutes, until light and fluffy.
4. Add the egg and vanilla extract and mix well until combined. Make sure to scrape down any mixture that sticks to the sides.
5. If using an electric food mixer, remove the bowl at this stage and continue mixing the mixture using a large metal spoon.
6. Add the flour, baking soda, cocoa powder, espresso powder and salt. Mix in all the ingredients gently, until everything has been mixed in.
7. Fold in the chocolate chips.
8. Using an ice cream scooper, scoop out cookie dough mix onto the prepared cookie sheet, leaving them 4cm apart.
9. Bake at 170°C for 12 minutes.
10. When done, remove from the oven and allow to cool completely on the baking sheet until set.
11. Enjoy!

You can also make these as triple chocolate cookies by simply adding white chocolate chips as well.

FRUIT & STEM GINGER FLORENTINES

Contrary to widely held belief, Florentines are not Italian, but French. It appears that these cookies were made for Catherine de Medici of Florence who marred Henry II of France. The 17th Century monarch commissioned the palace chefs to create a culinary delight to acknowledge their appreciation and admiration of the Medici family. Florentines are a sweet, thin cookie made with nuts and fruit and often half coated with chocolate. This is a simple recipe and the result is a delicious tasting fruity delight. I make these at Christmas and add cranberries and pistachios for a little festive colour.

Fruit & Stem Ginger Florentines

Makes approx. 8-12 Florentines

30g butter

75g golden caster sugar

15g plain flour

75ml creme fraîche

50g flaked almonds, toasted

25g dried cranberries

20g crystallised stem ginger

50g mixture of dried sour cherries & raisins

150g good quality dark chocolate, broken into pieces

acorn house
bakery

1. Preheat the oven to 180°C.
2. Heat the butter, sugar and flour in a pan over a medium heat, stirring continuously, until the butter has melted and the sugar has dissolved.
3. Gradually add the crème fraîche, stirring continuously until well combined.
4. Add the almonds, dried cranberries, stem ginger, sour cherries and raisins. Mix well until combined.
5. Line a baking tray with baking parchment or greaseproof paper and place teaspoonfuls of the florentine mixture onto it. Space the teaspoonfuls about 3cm apart, so that they don't merge together when baked.
6. Put in the oven and bake for 12-15 minutes, or until golden-brown. Remove from the oven and set aside to cool on the baking tray, then carefully transfer them to a cooling rack.
7. In a microwavable bowl, melt the dark chocolate pieces, heating it in 30sec intervals and stirring well each time. Stir until smooth and melted. Do not overheat.
8. Line the baking tray with a clean piece of packing parchment or greaseproof paper.
9. Turn the Florentines so that the flat base is facing upwards. Spread the melted chocolate over the Florentine bases and lay them, chocolate side down, on the lined baking tray. Set aside to cool and set.
10. Florentines may be served as they are or cut into shapes for making into gifts, eg hearts, stars or small circles. The off cuts can be kept and eaten as an indulgent snack!

These also make pretty, edible festive gifts when packaged in cellophane bags and tied with ribbon.

FRUIT & NUT CLUSTERS

These are my go-to indulgent snack recipe. This recipe is very simple to follow and there is no right way or wrong way to make your 'cluster' look – it is totally up to you. Whichever shape or size you make, the end result will always be delicious. The chocolate is decadent and the fruit and nut makes it a great indulgent snack you can have at any time. Try playing around with your favourite nut selection.

Fruit & Nut Clusters

Makes 15-18 clusters

155g mixture of blanched almonds/pistachios/chopped walnuts
50g mixture of dried fruits; sultanas/golden raisins/cranberries
100g dark chocolate (min. 50% cocoa solids), coarsley chopped
3 tbsp honey
Pinch of sea salt

acorn house
bakery

1. Preheat oven to 180°C.
2. Line a baking tray with greaseproof paper. Line another baking tray with greaseproof paper and set aside.
3. Sprinkle the nuts with the salt and scatter on to one of the baking trays and roast in the oven for 10-12 minutes.
4. While nuts are roasting, place chopped chocolate in a medium heatproof bowl. Place over a saucepan of barely simmering water to melt the chocolate. DO NOT ALLOW BOWL TO TOUCH THE WATER. Alternatively, you can melt the chocolate gently on medium power in a microware, heating it up for 30 seconds at a time, stirring in between. If the chocolate is heated too much and becomes too hot, it will cause 'blooming', which will give the finished result of your chocolate a white powdery look. Although unsightly, the chocolate is perfectly OK to eat!
5. Remove from the heat when most of the chocolate has melted and keep stirring. You'll find that the heat of the bowl will be enough to melt the unmelted chocolate. If all the chocolate does not melt, return to the heat, for 30 second at a time, stirring each time.
6. When the nuts are roasted, remove from the oven and set aside.
7. Once the chocolate has melted add the nuts, dried fruit and honey to the bowl and mix until combined.
8. Spoon the mixture (around 1 tbsp per cluster) onto the second greaseproof paper lined baking tray.
9. Allow chocolate to cool and solidify. This is best done overnight.
10. Once the clusters have set, place in a container and store in a cool place or in the fridge.

If you are not so keen on dark chcolate you can always use milk chocolate to make these treats.

AHB FRUITY BISCOTTI

Whenever you are travelling through Italy you will see these biscuits being served with coffee. These are an adaptation of those traditional Italian biscuits – I have added dried fruits.

I created this recipe when I wanted to serve them at Christmas. I added pistachios and dried cranberries for the green and red festive colours. This proved to be a hit and I have kept dried fruit in the recipe ever since.

You can swap the cranberries with golden raisins and/or sultanas. Either way, they make a nice fruity alternative to the traditional Italian version.

AHB Fruity Biscotti

Makes approx. 40-48 Biscotti

350g plain flour, plus extra for rolling

2 tsp baking powder

2 tsp mixed spice

250g golden caster sugar

3 eggs beaten

1 coarsely grated zest orange

85g golden raisins

85g dried cranberries

50g whole blanched almonds

50g shelled pistachios

acorn house
bakery

1. Heat oven to 170°C.
2. Line 2 baking sheets with baking paper.
3. Put the flour, baking powder, spice and sugar in a large bowl, then mix well.
4. Stir in the eggs and zest until the mixture starts forming clumps, then bring the dough together with your hands – it will seem dry at first but keep kneading until no floury patches remain.
5. Add the fruit and nuts, then work them in until evenly distributed.
6. Turn the dough out onto a lightly floured surface and divide into 4 pieces. With lightly floured hands, roll each piece into a sausage about 30cm long. Place 2 on each tray, well-spaced apart.
7. Bake for 25-30 mins until the dough has risen and spread and feels firm. It should still look pale.
8. Remove from the oven, transfer to a wire rack for a few mins until cool enough to handle.
9. Turn down the oven to 140°C.
10. Using a bread knife, cut into slices about 1cm thick on the diagonal, then lay the slices flat on the baking sheets. The biscuits can be cooled and frozen flat on the sheet at this point, then wrapped in cling film, bagged and frozen for up to 2 months.
11. Bake the cut biscuits for another 15 mins (if frozen, defrost first and cut up once thawed and then bake), turn over, then bake again for another 15 mins until dry and golden.
12. Tip onto a wire rack to cool completely, then store in an airtight tin for up to one month, or pack into boxes or cellophane bags tied with a ribbon and give as gifts.

These make beautiful edible gifts. You can make batches of these, package them up, tie with a ribbon and give as gifts for any occasion.

AHB CLASSIC SHORTBREAD

Shortbread is traditionally made into one of three shapes; a large circle for 'petticoat tails', small circles for 'shortbread rounds' or thick rectangular slabs for 'shortbread fingers'. I make mine as small rounds - it's easy and simple.
This recipe is great if you want to make biscuits at short notice. It really is quick and easy to make using just three ingredients. I like to make the batches of dough which I double wrap in cling film, pop in a freezer bag and put in the freezer. That way I always have some cookie dough available whenever I want to make some shortbread cookies.

AHB Classic Shortbread

Makes 12-16

375g plain flour

140g golden unrefined icing sugar (or light muscovado or soft brown sugar)

250g butter, chilled and cut into small pieces

½ tsp sea salt

Golden castor sugar (optional)

1. Heat oven to 170°C and line a baking tray with baking parchment or greaseproof paper.
2. Mix flour, icing sugar and salt together in a medium sized mixing bowl.
3. Add butter and mix together by rubbing the mixture between your fingers, until it comes together in a nice soft dough.
4. Lay a large sheet of parchment paper or cling film on a work surface. Place dough on top and cover with a similar sized sheet of parchment paper or cling film.
5. Roll out mixture in between these 2 sheets to about ½cm in thickness.
6. Cut out shapes required and place carefully on the baking tray. (Alternatively, you can place all of mixture smoothly into baking tray and mark lines on it so that it can be cut into squares after it is baked).
7. Use a fork to prick a few holes in the cookies.
8. Bake in oven for 18-22 minutes or until it is a pale brown colour.
9. When baked, remove from oven, carefully place on a cooling rack.
10. Cookies may be sprinkled with some golden castor sugar (if preferred), whilst warm.
11. Leave until cool.

Tips:

• Halfway through Step 3, you can add some flavours like: chocolate chips, chopped stem ginger or chopped pieces of glace cherries.

• These biscuits make a delicious simple dessert when served with strawberries (that have been halved and mixed with a little rum, Angostura's Bitters and golden icing sugar), and with a dollop of crème fraiche on the side.

• They also make great Christmas gifts when packaged up and tied with a festive bow.

Note: Biscuits will appear to be very soft when they come out of the oven. Resist the temptation to handle them too much, as they are likely to break when still hot.

You can actually flavour your shortbread with:
chocolate chips
chopped glacé cherries
chopped stem ginger
candied fruit

OREO BROWNIES

What chocolate lover does not like a brownie? These brownies take the ordinary traditional chocolate brownie to a new level. If you like chocolate and you like Oreo Cookies, then you will simply love these. Full of chocolatey yumminess, with the addition of irresistible Oreo Cookie pieces, this will more than satisfy any chocolate craving.

Oreo Cookies come in many different filling flavours, so why not try your favourite in this recipe instead?

Oreo Brownies

Makes 12 brownies

150g unsalted butter, melted

180g soft light brown sugar

150g caster sugar

3 large eggs

100g self-raising flour

50g cocoa powder

18-20 Oreo biscuits

1. Preheat your oven to 170°C.
2. Line an 20cm square tin with baking paper and set aside.
3. Put the melted butter into a large mixing bowl and add both sugars and whisk to combine.
4. Add in your eggs one at a time, mixing well between additions.
5. Sift in the flour and cocoa and stir in, using the whisk, until no streaks remain.
6. Pour just over half of the brownie mixture into your lined baking tin, spreading evenly.
7. Lay 16 Oreo biscuits in a layer over the brownie mix, pressing in gently to submerge slightly. Top with the rest of the brownie mix, making sure the Oreos are covered over.
8. Break up your remaining Oreos and gently push into the top of the brownie mixture.
9. Bake in your preheated oven for 25-35 minutes. Your brownies are done when the edges are firm and the middle has a crust but no wobble. Leave to cool in the baking tin.
10. When completely cool, cut into squares – whatever size you like - using a large sharp knife (dipped in hot water and wiped dry with kitchen paper), then simply enjoy!

These are great on their own, as an indulgent snack, or as a well-deserved dessert served warm with a dollop of crème fraîche or vanilla ice cream.

If you don't have Oreo Cookies, you can always use another chocolate sandwich biscuit or cookies as an alternative.

AHB HOMEMADE STRAWBERRY JAM

I love to use locally grown produce and Somerset does provide some delicious varieties of strawberry. Each year, without fail, I make my own strawberry jam. This is the fruitiest strawberry jam I have ever tasted! Strawberries are a traditional summer fruit to eat in the UK and when they are in season this is a wonderful way to savour the flavour throughout the year. Making jam is great when there is a glut of fruit at the end of the growing season. Even if you have never made jam before, just try it for yourself and see how easy it is to make. You won't be disappointed!

acorn house
bakery

AHB Homemade Jam

Makes 2 x 230g jars

500g strawberries
400g jam sugar
Juice of 1 lemon

acorn house bakery

1. Wash strawberries and cut in half. Place in a large bowl. Pour in jam sugar and mix well. Leave for a couple of hours to macerate.
2. Meanwhile, sterilise your jars and lids, by washing them in hot soapy water and rinsing them thoroughly with warm water. Then dry them in the oven set to 100°C for 15 minutes. Keep them warm.
3. Place a saucer in the freezer.
4. Transfer strawberry mixture to a large heavy bottomed high sided saucepan, add the lemon juice and gently heat to dissolve the sugar. Keep stirring the mixture until the sugar has dissolved.
5. When the sugar has dissolved, turn heat up to create a rolling boil of the mixture.
6. Boil for about 15-20 minutes until setting point (105°C) has been reached.
7. To test if it has reached setting point, place a teaspoon of the mixture onto the saucer from the freezer. Leave it for 2 minutes, then push your finger through the mixture. If it wrinkles the jam is done. If not, continue to boil the mixture for a few minutes more until it has set. Strawberry jam tends to be a soft set and therefore be a little runny in texture.
8. When done, remove from the heat and leave to settle for 10-15 minutes, skimming off any pink scum. This resting helps stop your fruit floating to the top of your jars!
9. Ladle the jam into the warm sterilised jars and seal.

Note: This jam will keep for at least 1 year if the jar is unopened. Once opened store in the fridge and consume within 6 weeks. Always use a clean spoon to take jam out of the jar!

Strawberries are low in pectin which is needed to make the jam set. However strawberry jam should be a little runny so don't be disappointed if it does not set thickly. Just make sure that you use jam sugar in this recipe.

CAKES, SPONGES & SCONES

BANANA & CHOCOLATE CHIP CAKE

Some people make banana bread, I make banana CAKE! Whenever bananas were over ripe at home, my mother would say, "Don't throw those out, I'll make a banana cake". This was like music to my ears because her banana cake was not to be missed. I recreated it several times when my children were growing up and added chocolate chips to the recipe which simply added to the deliciousness of this cake. It was definitely one of their favourites. You can also create an adult version by adding 2-3 tbsp of rum to the cake mixture before baking. You can use either dark or white rum as both work really well.

Banana & Chocolate Chip Cake

Serves 6-8

170g butter, softened

170g demerara granulated sugar

3 large eggs

2 very ripe bananas, mashed

1 firm banana, for decoration

170g self-raising flour

100g ground almonds

1 tsp baking powder

1 tsp vanilla extract

¼ tsp salt

80g dark chocolate chips

1. Pre-heat oven to 170°C.
2. Grease and flour well a 22cm cake tin or 900g loaf tin.
3. In a large mixing bowl, using an electric whisk, mix together butter, sugar, flour, baking powder and eggs, until well combined. Can also be mixed together using a wooden spoon.
4. Using a wooden spoon, stir in ground almonds.
5. Then stir in mashed bananas and vanilla essence. Mix well, until you have a lovely smooth consistency. If mixture is too runny, you can add an additional teaspoon or two of self-raising flour.
6. Gently stir in the chocolate chips.
7. Pour batter into the cake tin. Slice the firm banana into disks and arrange on top of the batter.
8. Bake for 1 hour, or until cake tester (or bamboo skewer) comes out clean.
9. When cooked, remove from oven and allow to rest for 10mins, before turning out onto a cooling rack to completely cool.
10. Serve warm or cool, with vanilla ice cream, crème fraiche or custard.

Tip:
You can stir in 50ml of dark rum after adding the dry ingredients, for a decadent banana and chocolate chip cake.

This is a very moist cake, therefore the mixture, before you put it into the cake tin, may be slightly runny
– this is OK!

If you have a nut allergy, leave out the ground almonds and substitute them with the equivalent weight in self-raising flour.

CARIBBEAN RUM FRUIT CAKE

This recipe was handed down to me from my mother who made this cake without fail every Christmas but also for celebrations. It requires the dried fruits to be soaked in dark rum up to a month before the cake is baked, allowing them to soften and take on the rum's rich caramel flavours. The infused fruit gives the cake a delicious moist texture when eaten. My mother always used dark rum from Guyana (her birthplace). This method of soaking fruits is the definition of a rich fruit cake and they can last for a long time. Wrap in cling film then tin foil and store in a cool dark place in an airtight container.

Caribbean Rum Fruit Cake

Makes 1 x 15cm round cake

100g butter, softened

100g soft dark brown sugar

30g Blackstrap molasses

2 large eggs

125g plain flour, sifted

1 tsp ground cinnamon

1 tbsp mixed spice

450g mixed dried fruit, previously soaked in 150ml dark Caribbean rum for at 3-4 weeks*

3 tbsp dark Caribbean rum

acorn house
bakery

1. Pre-heat the oven to 150°C.
2. Line a 15cm round cake tin with 2 layers of baking parchment.
3. In a large bowl, mix the softened butter and soft brown sugar with an electric hand mixer until it is a nice creamy texture. This should take about 2 minutes.
4. Add the molasses and mix in evenly, using the electric hand mixer.
5. Add the eggs, mixing in one at a time, using the electric hand mixer. They do not have to be perfectly mixed in. Avoid over beating the eggs.
6. Using a wooden spoon, gently stir the spices and half of the flour into the mixture.
7. Using a wooden spoon, stir half of the soaked fruits into the mixture.
8. Stir the remaining flour and soaked fruits into the mixture. Stir until all the flour has been mixed in.
9. Spoon the mixture into the prepared cake tin and bake for 1½ hours. Check that the cake has cooked completely by inserting a bamboo skewer into the centre. If it comes out clean, the cake is cooked. It is it still uncooked, bake for a further 10 minutes and do the test again. Repeat if further baking is required.
10. Remove cake from the oven when cooked and pour the 3 tbsp of dark rum over it, while it is still hot.
11. Leave the cake in the tin and cover loosely with tin foil, with a clean tea towel over it.
12. Allow the cake to cool completely before removing from the tin.
13. The cake can be eaten as it is or decorated in any way you want.
14. Store the cake in an airtight container.

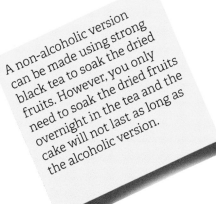

A non-alcoholic version can be made using strong black tea to soak the dried fruits. However, you only need to soak the dried fruits overnight in the tea and the cake will not last as long as the alcoholic version.

GIN & TONIC LEMON DRIZZLE CAKE

Lemon drizzle cake is a favourite with many as a tea time treat or as part of an afternoon tea selection. There are many versions varying from those with a lemony syrup poured over them to those with a crunchy lemon flavoured icing on top. This recipe is my adult version of this classic teatime favourite. It takes the humble lemon drizzle cake to another level. The zingyness of the drizzle with the kick of the gin makes this cake a superior addition to an afternoon tea cake selection. This cake is great as an afternoon treat or made and decorated for a special occasion.

Gin & Tonic Lemon Drizzle Cake

Serves 6 - 8

For the cake: (for a 900g loaf tin)

200g softened unsalted butter, plus extra for greasing

175g caster sugar

4 medium eggs

200g self-raising flour, sifted

½ tsp baking powder

1 finely grated zest unwaxed lemon

75ml gin

For the syrup:

150g caster sugar

30ml tonic water

20ml lemon juice

3 tbsp gin

For the icing and decoration:

200g icing sugar

30ml lemon

1 tbsp gin

Candied Lemon & Lime Slices (optional) - can be made in advance: Take ½ lemon & ½ lime. Thinly sliced (about 3mm tick) , with a mandolin or sharp knife. Add 200ml water, 200g granulated sugar and 30ml lemon juice to a saucepan. Over a low heat, stir to dissolve the sugar, then bring to the boil for 1 min. Lower heat to a simmer and add lemon and lime slices in a single layer. Simmer for 15mins, turning slices occasionally. When the slices are translucent it's done. If not, simmer until they become translucent.
Remove the slices and lay them on a baking parchment lined baking tray. They can be left out to dry overnight or placed in an oven heated to 90°C for about an hour or until they have stiffened up. Allow to cool before using.

acorn house
bakery

1. Preheat the oven to 160°C.

2. Grease with butter and line a 900g loaf tin with baking parchment. Make sure the baking parchment is at least 3cm higher than the tin.

3. Put the butter and sugar into a bowl, and whisk with an electric whisk until pale, light, and fluffy.

4. Lightly beat the eggs in a jug. Then, pour them, a little at a time, into the butter and sugar mixture, mixing them in each time with a wooden spoon.

5. Gently fold in the flour, baking powder, and lemon zest. The batter should be slightly runny.

6. Pour in the gin and give it a gentle stir. Spoon into the prepared tin.

7. Bake for 45mins to an hour. After 40 minutes, insert a bamboo skewer (or cake tester) into the centre of the cake and, if it comes out clean, the cake is done. If it doesn't, bake it for a further 5 minutes. Test again.

8. Meanwhile, make the syrup. Put the sugar, tonic water and lemon juice into a small pan over a low heat and stir gently until the sugar dissolves. When completely dissolved, increase the heat and boil the syrup for about 2 minutes without stirring, until it starts to reduce and thicken. Remove pan from the heat and add the gin.

9. Once the cake is out of the oven, but still warm, use a skewer to make several holes on the top.

10. Generously drizzle the gin syrup over the top of the cake and leave to cool in the tin.

11. Remove the cake from the tin, and place on a wire rack.

12. Make the icing, gradually adding the lemon juice and gin alternately to the icing sugar, until you have a runny consistency. Spoon the mixture evenly over the cake.

13. Arrange the lemon slices along the top. Leave to set.

If you do not want to use alcohol, try substituting it with some elderflower cordial, which compliments the lemon very well.

MOIST GINGER CAKE

Ginger is an ingredient used quite a lot in Caribbean cooking, especially baking. Both fresh ginger and ground ginger were used a lot in my mother's cooking, whether it was a savoury or a sweet dish.

One of my childhood favourites that my mother used to make was a rich and sticky ginger cake, moist and dark with molasses. The addition of the stem ginger pieces makes this a cake that you can have with a cup of tea or coffee, or as we used to have it as kids, served warm with custard! It can also be served warm as a dessert with crème fraiche.

Moist Ginger Cake

Serves 6 - 8

Cake:
115g butter
75ml molasses (Blackstrap is best) or treacle
2 large eggs
150g self-raising flour
1 tsp baking powder
120g soft brown sugar or dark Muscovado sugar
75g stem ginger, chopped into small pieces
1tbsp ground ginger
½ tsp ground cinnamon

Syrup:
75g golden caster sugar
2 tsp ground ginger
50ml water

Decoration (optional):
130g icing sugar
20ml lemon juice
1 ball of stem ginger, sliced or chopped
into small pieces

acorn house
bakery

1. Heat oven to 170°C. Grease and line 900g loaf tin with baking parchment.
2. Gently warm butter, treacle together in a saucepan, just enough to melt the butter.
3. When melted, remove from the heat, add eggs and stir together briskly with a whisk. Set aside.
4. In a large mixing bowl, sift flour, bicarbonate of soda, baking powder and spices and mix together with a wooden spoon. Stir in the sugar, using the wooden spoon.
5. Add the chopped stem ginger and mix in.
6. Add the wet liquid to the dry ingredients and, using a wooden spoon, mix together until well combined.
7. Pour into prepared loaf tin and bake for about 50min, or more if needed, until thoroughly cooked. To test if the cake is cooked, insert a bamboo skewer or cake tester. If it comes out clean the cake is cooked, if not, bake for a little longer.
8. Whilst the cake in baking, make the syrup. Mix the sugar and ground ginger together and place in a saucepan with the water. Heat through, stirring all the time, until all the sugar has dissolved. Bring to a vigorous boil and simmer over a very low heat for 5mins. Keep warm.
9. When the cake is cooked, remove from the oven, prick the top a few times with a cocktail stick and pour the warm syrup over the hot cake.
10. Place the baking tin, with the cake still in it, on a cooling rack and allow to cool for 10mins. When cool, remove cake from baking tin and allow to cool completely on a cooling rack.
11. If decorating, sift the icing sugar and mix in the lemon juice. Place the cake on a serving plate and pour the icing over the cake allowing it to drip down the sides. Decorate with slices/pieces of stem ginger.

Try adding a few pieces of chopped dates, instead of, or as well as the chopped stem ginger pieces.

PEAR & ALMOND CAKE

I grow two varieties of pear in my Somerset garden and use either of them in this recipe, but you can use any firm pear like Conference, William or even a Comice.

This light sponge cake could be mistaken for being a cross between a cake and a pudding – but who cares, it's yummy either way! The ground almonds give a great moist texture to this cake and the pears, a fruity balance.

This cake works well as an afternoon treat or as a delicious dessert served warm or cold with custard or ice cream.

acorn house
bakery

Pear & Almond Cake

Serves 6-8

300g firm pears (any type of sweet pear will do)

2 tbsp lemon juice

115g caster sugar

115g butter softened

2 eggs, beaten

40g ground almonds

75g self-raising flour

1 tsp almond extract

½ tsp ground cinnamon

½ tsp baking powder

10g flaked almonds

1. Preheat the oven to 170°C.

2. Line a round 20cm cake tin with baking parchment.

3. Peel, core and cut the pears into quarters. Take one pear quarter and chop it into very small pieces and place in a small bowl. Pour over 1 tsp of the lemon juice and sprinkle with a little ground cinnamon. Give it a stir to mix it up. This will be mixed into the cake mixture before baking.

4. Slice the remaining quarters into 3 thin slices each. Place in another bowl and pour over the remaining lemon juice and sprinkle with the rest of the ground cinnamon and 1 tsp of the caster sugar. Mix well and set aside.

5. In a large mixing bowl, add all the remaining caster sugar, softened butter, eggs, ground almonds, self-raising flour, baking powder and almond extract. DO NOT add the flaked almonds.

6. Mix all the ingredients together with an electric hand mixer or wooden spoon, until well combined.

7. Strain the small pieces of pear and gently stir the pieces of pear into the mixture, until well combined.

8. Spoon the mixture into the lined cake tin and level the surface with a palette knife or the back of a spoon.

9. Drain any juices from the sliced pears and arrange the pear slices in a circular pattern on the top of the mixture.

10. Sprinkle the flaked almonds on top.

11. Put in the oven and bake for about 45-50 minutes until cooked. The cake is done when a wooden skewer inserted into the centre comes out clean and when you can see that the sides have come away from the edge of the cake tin.

12. Run a knife around the edge of the cake and leave to cool in the tin for 10 minutes before transferring to a wire rack to cool completely.

13. To serve, sprinkle with some icing sugar, and eat as a piece of cake or warm with crème fraîche as a dessert!

Note: You will need several bowls for this recipe but the end result is worth it!

SOMERSET CIDER APPLE CAKE

You will find that in most apple growing counties there is some kind of apple cake, and Somerset is not an exception. Living in Somerset you can never go far without seeing apples or cider.
So this cake is fitting as a homage to my home county. I have used the John Grieve apples grown in my garden, but you can use any firm and tart, sweet tasting apple, such as Cox's, Gala or Braeburn. I have also used Somerset cider – obviously!
Apple cake are traditional culinary symbols of the UK's West Country counties, giving us Dorset apple cake, Devonshire apple cake and Somerset apple cake.

Somerset Cider Apple Cake

Serves 8-10

175g sultanas

150ml dry Somerset cider

280g self-raising flour

½ tsp baking powder

1 tsp ground cinnamon

½ tsp mixed spice

1 pinch salt

225g golden caster sugar

180g salted butter

3 eggs, beaten

3 large firm apples, cored and peeled

1 tbsp lemon juice

2 tbsp Somerset apple brandy

30g flaked almonds

1 tbsp demerara sugar

1. Set oven to 170°C.
2. Grease a 20cm round cake tin and line with baking parchment.
3. Put the cider in a small saucepan and add the sultanas, bring to the boil, lower the heat and simmer over a low heat for about 15 minutes.
4. Slice the apples thinly. Place them in a small mixing bowl, then pour the 2 tablespoons of brandy and lemon juice over them and mix well. Cover the bowl with a plate. Set aside.
5. Sieve the flour, baking powder, salt and spices into a medium sized mixing bowl.
6. In a separate large mixing bowl, cream the sugar and butter with an electric hand mixer, until pale and fluffy. Add the eggs to the mixture, a little at a time, and mix in well.
7. Add the dry ingredients (except the flaked almonds) to the wet mixture and fold in using a wooden spoon.
8. Set aside about 12-15 slices of the sliced apple in a small bowl and add the remaining sliced apples to the mixture and fold in gently.
9. Stir in the soaked sultanas, along with the juices from the soaked apple slices.
10. Spoon the mixture into the lined tin and smooth over the top with the back of a spoon, to make it even on top.
11. Arrange the remaining sliced apples, that you set aside, over the top of the mixture.
12. Sprinkle the flaked almonds and demerara sugar over the top and bake for about 45-50 minutes, or until an inserted bamboo skewer comes out clean.
13. Cool in the tin for 10 minutes, then turn out onto a wire cooling rack until completely cool.
14. This cake may be served at room temperature as a cake or warm with crème fraiche mixed with a little brandy!

You can use pears as an alternative to the apples and pear cider as a substitute for the apple cider.

THE ULTIMATE AHB SCONES

This recipe makes the traditional scone bolder and better. The added natural yoghurt gives the scones extra yumminess. But don't take our word for it, try it yourself!!

When eating our scones, we recommend spreading the jam first and then adding a dollop of clotted cream – the Cornish way.

The Ultimate AHB Scones

Makes 8-10 large scones

450g strong white flour

2 tsp baking powder

pinch salt

90g caster sugar

80g butter, diced and cold

200ml full fat milk

100g natural live yoghurt

½ tsp vanilla extract

1 egg yolk, mixed with ½ tsp of water for the egg wash

To serve:

Strawberry jam (see AHB Homemade Jam recipe ~ page 121)

Clotted cream

1. Preheat the oven to 210°C.
2. Line a baking tray with baking parchment.
3. Put the flour, sugar, salt and baking powder in a large mixing bowl and stir the dry ingredients together, using a wooden spoon.
4. Add the butter and using your fingertips rub the mixture until it resembles breadcrumbs. Set aside.
5. Stir the yoghurt into the milk, add the vanilla extract and mix together.
6. Make a well in the centre of the dry ingredients and pour in the milk and yoghurt mixture. Mix together using a large fork or spoon, until you have a rough dough. Then use your hands (lightly floured) to bring it all together into a smooth ball of dough.
7. Roll out the dough on a lightly floured surface until it is about 3cm in thickness. Cut out circles using a 7cm – 8cm round cookie cutter. If you don't have a cookie cutter, you can use a glass or teacup, but make sure to dust the edge in flour before cutting out the circles so that the dough does not get stuck in the glass or cup.
8. Place the circles of dough onto the baking tray, and using your fingers, gently ease the top edge of the dough upwards.
9. Brush the tops with the egg wash, using a pastry brush (or your finger).
10. Bake for 15 to 18 minutes, until golden brown.
11. When baked, remove from the oven and cool on a cooling rack.
12. To serve, split in half horizontally and spread with jam and a dollop of clotted cream.

Try this decadent variation of our AHB scones: replace the sultanas with dark chocolate chips and the jam with chocolate spread for the ultimate chocoholic cream tea!

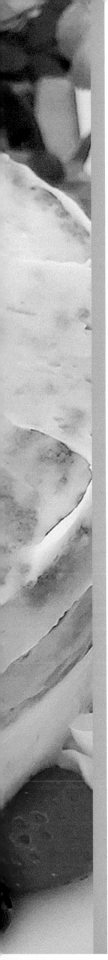

AHB VICTORIA SPONGE

The Victoria Sponge is quintessentially English and the most popular cake eaten in the UK today. It is said that the sponge cake was Queen Victoria's favourite cake, however it was after the death of her husband, Prince Albert, in 1861, that the Victoria Sponge Cake was named in her honour. Traditionally, the two sponges that make the cake were sandwiched together with just jam; it was in later years that whipped cream or buttercream was also added before they were sandwiched and became the cake we know today. In this recipe I use my homemade Strawberry Jam, but you can use whichever jam you prefer.

AHB Victoria Sponge

Serves 8-10

200g caster sugar

200g salted butter, softened

4 eggs, beaten

200g self-raising flour

1 tsp baking powder

½ tsp vanilla extract

30ml full fat milk

For the Filling:

100g butter, softened

140g golden unrefined icing sugar, sifted (if not available, use normal icing sugar)

½ tsp vanilla extract (if using normal icing sugar)

150g strawberry (or your preferred) jam (see AHB Homemade Jam recipe ~ page 121)

Icing sugar, to decorate

1. Heat oven to 170°C.
2. Grease and line two 20cm sandwich tins with baking parchment.
3. In a large bowl, beat all the cake ingredients together with an electric hand mixer until you have a smooth, soft batter.
4. Divide the mixture between the tins, smoothing the surface with a spatula or the back of a spoon
5. Bake for about 20 minutes until golden and the cake has come away from the sides of the baking tins and springs back when pressed.
6. Leave in the tins to cool for 10 minutes, then turn out onto a cooling rack and leave to cool completely.
7. To make the filling, beat the butter until smooth and creamy, then gradually beat in icing sugar.
8. Beat in vanilla extract, if using.
9. Spread the buttercream over the top of one of the cooled sponges, top it with strawberry jam and sandwich the second sponge on top.
10. Dust with a little icing sugar before serving or if you're feeling adventurous, you could spread some buttercream over the top and all around the side of the cake and decorate with some fresh strawberries.
11. May be kept in an airtight container in a cool place for up to 2 days, or in the fridge up to a week.

Making homemade jam is surprisingly easy. Try my recipe for Strawberry Jam on page 121.

Author Bio

Helen was born to Guyanese parents in South East London, where she grew up in a large household. She remembers well her mother and grandmother baking bread and cakes at home; the family favourites being plaited loaf and rum-laced fruit cake.

After finishing her education, Helen began work in a publishing company and later spent three years in Hong Kong with her husband when their two children were very young. On returning to London, Helen completed her MBA and worked for several years in the technology world before deciding to retrain at the Westminster Kingsway College and Le Cordon Bleu School in London.

When the family relocated to South Somerset, Helen took the opportunity to focus on her baking and became skilled in making and decorating celebration cakes, speciality cookies, chocolate and confectionery. She went on to set up Acorn House Bakery in 2021 so that she could specialise in luxury treat boxes filled with personalised artisanal cookies, chocolates and fudge. Today Helen sells her baked goods along with her own recipe artisanal jams, marmalades and chutneys at local country fairs and markets. She loves to use fruit grown from her own kitchen garden as well as locally grown produce.

Outside of baking Helen enjoys international travel, particularly when she can learn more about the different ways food can be enjoyed from around the world. She has also been privileged to work as a sitting magistrate in London andlatterly on the Wiltshire bench for some 25 years.

With these recipes inspired by Helen's childhood memories and her passion for baking she is delighted to be able to share this wonderful collection - which comes right from her heart.

Index